discarded

OBSESSIVE-COMPULSIVE DISORDER

MENTAL ILLNESSES AND DISORDERS

MENTAL ILLNESSES AND DISORDERS
Awareness and Understanding

OBSESSIVE-COMPULSIVE DISORDER

H.W. Poole

SERIES CONSULTANT
ANNE S. WALTERS, PhD
Chief Psychologist, Emma Pendleton Bradley Hospital
Clinical Associate Professor, Alpert Medical School/Brown University

MASON CREST

Mason Crest
450 Parkway Drive, Suite D
Broomall, PA 19008
www.masoncrest.com

MTM Publishing, Inc.
435 West 23rd Street, #8C
New York, NY 10011
www.mtmpublishing.com

President: Valerie Tomaselli
Vice President, Book Development: Hilary Poole
Designer: Annemarie Redmond
Copyeditor: Peter Jaskowiak
Editorial Assistant: Andrea St. Aubin

Series ISBN: 978-1-4222-3364-1
ISBN: 978-1-4222-3373-3
Ebook ISBN: 978-1-4222-8574-9

Library of Congress Cataloging-in-Publication Data
Poole, Hilary W., author.
  Obsessive-compulsive disorder / by H.W. Poole.
     pages cm. — (Mental illnesses and disorders : awareness and understanding)
  Includes bibliographical references and index.
  ISBN 978-1-4222-3373-3 (hardback) — ISBN 978-1-4222-3364-1 (series) — ISBN
978-1-4222-8574-9 (ebook)
  1. Obsessive-compulsive disorder—Juvenile literature. 2. Anxiety disorders—Juvenile
literature. I. Title.
  RC533.P66 2016
  616.85'227—dc23
                                                                              2015006705

Printed and bound in the United States of America.

9 8 7 6 5 4 3 2

TABLE OF CONTENTS

Key Icons to Look for:

Words to Understand: These words with their easy-to-understand definitions will increase the reader's understanding of the text, while building vocabulary skills.

Sidebars: This boxed material within the main text allows readers to build knowledge, gain insights, explore possibilities, and broaden their perspectives by weaving together additional information to provide realistic and holistic perspectives.

Research Projects: Readers are pointed toward areas of further inquiry connected to each chapter. Suggestions are provided for projects that encourage deeper research and analysis.

Text-Dependent Questions: These questions send the reader back to the text for more careful attention to the evidence presented there.

Series Glossary of Key Terms: This back-of-the-book glossary contains terminology used throughout the series. Words found here increase the reader's ability to read and comprehend higher-level books and articles in this field.

People who cope with mental illnesses and disorders deserve our empathy and respect.

Introduction to the Series

According to the National Institute of Mental Health, in 2012 there were an estimated 45 million people in the United States suffering from mental illness, or 19 percent of all US adults. A separate 2011 study found that among children, almost one in five suffer from some form of mental illness or disorder. The nature and level of impairment varies widely. For example, children and adults with anxiety disorders may struggle with a range of symptoms, from a constant state of worry about both real and imagined events to a complete inability to leave the house. Children or adults with schizophrenia might experience periods when the illness is well controlled by medication and therapies, but there may also be times when they must spend time in a hospital for their own safety and the safety of others. For every person with mental illness who makes the news, there are many more who do not, and these are the people that we must learn more about and help to feel accepted, and even welcomed, in this world of diversity.

It is not easy to have a mental illness in this country. Access to mental health services remains a significant issue. Many states and some private insurers have "opted out" of providing sufficient coverage for mental health treatment. This translates to limits on the amount of sessions or frequency of treatment, inadequate rates for providers, and other problems that make it difficult for people to get the care they need.

Meanwhile, stigma about mental illness remains widespread. There are still whispers about "bad parenting," or "the other side of the tracks." The whisperers imply that mental illness is something you bring upon yourself, or something that someone does to you. Obviously, mental illness can be exacerbated by an adverse event such as trauma or parental instability. But there is just as much truth to the biological bases of mental illness. No one is made schizophrenic by ineffective parenting, for example, or by engaging in "wild" behavior as an adolescent. Mental illness is a complex interplay of genes, biology, and the environment, much like many physical illnesses.

People with mental illness are brave soldiers, really. They fight their illness every day, in all of the settings of their lives. When people with an anxiety disorder graduate from college, you know that they worked very hard to get there—harder, perhaps, than those who did not struggle with a psychiatric issue. They got up every day with a pit in their stomach about facing the world, and they worried about their finals more than their classmates. When they had to give a presentation in class, they thought their world was going to end and that they would faint, or worse, in front of everyone. But they fought back, and they kept going. Every day. That's bravery, and that is to be respected and congratulated.

These books were written to help young people get the facts about mental illness. Facts go a long way to dispel stigma. Knowing the facts gives students the opportunity to help others to know and understand. If your student lives with someone with mental illness, these books can help students know a bit more about what to expect. If they are concerned about someone, or even about themselves, these books are meant to provide some answers and a place to start.

The topics covered in this series are those that seem most relevant for middle schoolers—disorders that they are most likely to come into contact with or to be curious about. Schizophrenia is a rare illness, but it is an illness with many misconceptions and inaccurate portrayals in media. Anxiety and depressive disorders, on the other hand, are quite common. Most of our youth have likely had personal experience of anxiety or depression, or knowledge of someone who struggles with these symptoms.

As a teacher or a librarian, thank you for taking part in dispelling myths and bringing facts to your children and students. Thank you for caring about the brave soldiers who live and work with mental illness. These reference books are for all of them, and also for those of us who have the good fortune to work with and know them.

—Anne S. Walters, PhD
Chief Psychologist, Emma Pendleton Bradley Hospital
Clinical Professor, Alpert Medical School/Brown University

CHAPTER ONE

THE DOUBTING DISEASE

Words to Understand

antibodies: substances produced by the human body to attack viruses and infections.

compulsion: the strong need to complete an action.

intrusive: unwelcome and annoying.

obsession: an idea that a person cannot force out of his or her mind, even if he or she wants to.

plateau: a stable, level place.

ritual: an activity that is repeated again and again in the same way.

Even when people with OCD "know" that nothing bad will happen if they don't do their rituals, they still *feel* like something will.

Imagine that you are trying to fall asleep one night. Suddenly, you wonder if the front door is locked. You get out of bed to check the door. Yes, it's locked. So you go back to bed and fall asleep. Simple, right?

For some people, life is not that simple.

Even after the door is checked, a different person might think, "Wait, is it *really* locked?" He needs to check it again. And again.

He tells himself, "I know the door is locked! I won't get up again." But bad thoughts start to run through his mind. "What if it isn't really locked? What if a murderer kills me and my family while we sleep?" These terrible thoughts force him to get up and check the door.

This person doesn't want to get up again and again. He wants to go to sleep just like you did. But he feels he *must* check that door again, because bad things will happen if he doesn't.

Habits and Rituals

Lots of us have little **rituals** we like to do. Maybe you always wear special socks when you have a soccer game. Or maybe you always put your markers back in the box in rainbow order—

Some people need things to be put away in the exact same order every time. It's not necessarily a case of OCD.

FAMOUS PEOPLE WITH OCD

Having OCD will not prevent you from achieving great things. Historians suspect that many important people from history might have some form of the disorder, including:

- Ludwig van Beethoven, composer
- Sir Winston Churchill, politician
- Charles Darwin, scientist
- Albert Einstein, scientist
- Howard Hughes, businessman
- Samuel Johnson, writer
- Michelangelo, artist
- Nicola Tesla, scientist

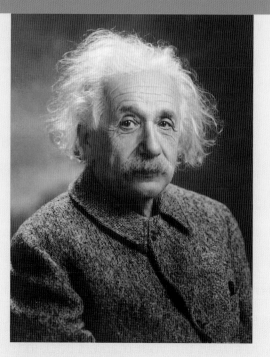

Albert Einstein.

it has to be red, orange, yellow, green, blue, and purple. Before taking a test, maybe you tap your desk for good luck.

You may not know exactly *why* you do these things. It just "feels right" to do them. And there is nothing wrong with little rituals like these. Unique habits are part of what make people so interesting!

But what if one of your favorite socks went missing, and you got *so* upset that you couldn't play in the game at all? What if you couldn't sleep at night because you kept worrying that the yellow marker had been put in the wrong spot? What if you needed to tap your desk 30 times before every test, and in a certain pattern? And if someone interrupted you, you had to start all over from the beginning? Your ritual would no longer be fun—it would be a problem.

What Is OCD?

At the beginning of the chapter, we talked about someone who could not stop wondering if the door was locked. That nagging thought is called an **obsession**. The act of checking the door again and again is a **compulsion**. That is why we say this person has obsessive-compulsive disorder (OCD).

OCD is a mental disorder involving **intrusive** thoughts and rituals that have a negative effect on the person who has them. Let's say you have a video game collection and you want the games arranged in a certain way. That's not necessarily a problem—even if other people don't understand why you arrange them. But if arranging the games becomes something you think about a *lot*, and if it prevents you from completing other activities, that can be a problem. OCD involves thoughts and rituals that are upsetting and make daily life difficult.

Washing and rewashing hands is a classic OCD ritual.

PANDAS

It may seem strange, but a throat infection called strep can sometimes trigger OCD in certain kids. Doctors are not certain why this happens, but they do have a theory. When you get sick, your body produces **antibodies** to attack the disease. And it seems that sometimes the antibodies go too far, and they begin attacking parts of the brain. Kids who have never shown signs of OCD can develop it very quickly. This type of OCD is called PANDAS, which stands for Pediatric Autoimmune Neuropsychiatric Disorders Associated with Streptococcal Infections.

It's important to understand that while strep is very common, PANDAS is not. And it often gets better over time, as the antibodies end their attack.

Intrusive thoughts and rituals can be different for every person. But there are some things people with OCD often do. Hand-washing is one common ritual, and so is putting objects in a specific order. Another is counting—for example, someone might count the number of steps she takes. Checking and rechecking something, as with our locked door example, is another common compulsion.

Some people with OCD can't stop thinking that something terrible is about to happen—they believe they are about to get hurt or that they are about to hurt someone else. Or they are sure they will catch a disease. Other people with OCD ask the same questions over and over, looking for reassurance from others. No matter how many times the question is answered, it never seems to help.

The behaviors—checking or washing or asking—do slow down or stop for certain periods. People with OCD can reach a **plateau** where they feel like they have done the ritual enough. Maybe the person in our door-checking example will be able to stop checking after 20 times or 30 times. But he'll have lost a lot of sleep at that point! He'll probably be very frustrated. Soon, the compulsion will return, and he will have to start checking again.

Knowing What You Know

The French term for OCD is *folie de doute*, or "the doubting disease." That's because constant, nagging worry is a big part of the disorder.

Having OCD can make it extremely difficult to finish homework, because you never feel certain that it's done correctly.

Take the locked-door example from the beginning of the chapter. For most of us, seeing that the door is locked is enough. We know that the door is locked, so we stop thinking about it. But people with OCD have difficulty knowing that they know certain things. Here is another example. Most people wash their hands and know that they are clean. But someone with OCD might need to wash her hands again and again, because her mind doesn't "know" that they are clean already.

People with OCD can't "know" certain things, no matter how many times they look at the evidence. But that doesn't mean they aren't smart. In fact, many people with OCD are *very* smart! They have no trouble knowing lots of other things. But OCD seems to target certain kinds of knowledge in certain people.

Researchers do not know for sure why some people develop OCD, but they believe that the condition may run in families.

Who Gets OCD?

As mentioned earlier, lots of us have rituals, but we don't all have OCD. Why do some people develop the disorder while

others do not? No one knows for sure, but there are a number of theories about possible causes.

- *Brain structure and chemistry*. The brains of people with OCD may simply not work quite the same as those of other people.
- *Heredity*. OCD tends to run in families. People who have relatives with OCD are more likely to develop it themselves.
- *Childhood illness*. There may be a connection between the common illness strep throat and having OCD (see box). A brain injury could also be a cause.

Whatever causes it, OCD is not an easy disorder to live with. However, lots of people with OCD learn how to manage the condition. In later chapters, we will talk about how OCD is treated and discuss tips on coping. First, let's look at some other disorders that are closely related to OCD.

Text-Dependent Questions

1. What are some common rituals of people with OCD?
2. Name the theories about what might cause OCD.

Research Project

Study the life of one of the famous people with OCD listed in the box. Did the disorder help or hurt their work? Or both? How? (You might start with a biography of one of the people listed on page 12. Or check out the "Famous People with OCD" page on the New Health Guide website, at www. newhealthguide.org/famous-people-with-OCD.html.)

CHAPTER TWO

OCD-RELATED DISORDERS

Words to Understand

anxiety: a feeling of worry or nervousness.

betrayal: going against a person or belief.

discoloration: a change in the normal color of something.

repetitive: something that happens over and over again.

The rituals of someone with OCD don't always stay the same. At first, a person might feel compelled to check the front door, but over time he might become more obsessed with washing or counting. The intrusive thoughts can change over time.

But there are some disorders related to OCD that tend to stay very focused. Some center around the person's body, while others center on the person's living conditions.

Body Obsessions

Some people with OCD-related disorders become very focused on their own bodies.

Body Dysmorphic Disorder (BDD). A person with BDD is extremely focused on an imagined physical flaw in her body.

People with body dysmorphic disorder become focused on physical "flaws" that usually don't matter to anyone else.

NAIL BITING

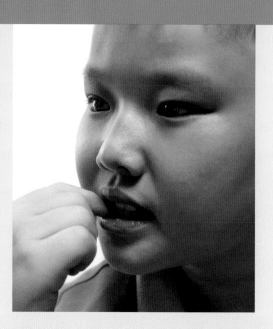

Biting your nails is a common habit. But it's never a good idea. First, you can easily bite or rip the nail too far back and hurt yourself. Also, whenever you bite your nails, you are putting dirt or germs you might have touched directly into your mouth.

A lot of us do it anyway, especially when we are nervous about something. Nail biting is considered a body-focused **repetitive** behavior, just like the disorders we are discussing here. But, unlike those disorders, nail biting is a pretty minor thing. However, severe nail biting can lead to **discoloration**, infection, and some gross-looking fingers. It is better to ease your anxiety some other way.

One common focus is on body weight. In fact, many people with eating disorders are also suffering from BDD. When they look in the mirror, they see a very fat person—even if they are starving themselves to death.

Weight is just one example of BDD. People with BDD might focus on their muscles, or their skin, or any "flaw" they see. No matter how much you might tell them that their bodies are fine, they can't believe you. People with BDD often avoid social situations, because they believe that other people are judging their "flaw." This can be a problem for kids, because having friends and going to school are such important parts of growing up.

Hair Pulling. The official term for this disorder is *trichotillomania (TTM).* That's quite a mouthful to say ("trick-o-till-o-MAY-nee-ah"), but it just means the desire to pull out your own hair. The Greek word for "hair" is *tricho,* and the verb "to pull" is *tillo.* People with TTM pull hair not only from their heads but also from their eyebrows, underarms, legs, or any other parts of their bodies. TTM can be mild or very severe. Severe cases can leave people with bald patches or infections.

Skin Picking. This disorder involves repetitive picking at the skin. Sometimes people pick to remove a bit of skin they find unattractive—if the person has acne, for example. Sometimes, though, people pick at their skin for no obvious reason. Usually, they are experiencing some level of **anxiety**, and the behavior makes them feel better for a time. Afterward, however, people with this disorder tend to feel very upset and embarrassed about what they've done. Severe picking can lead to skin damage, infections, and scars.

OCD MYTH

It is a myth that OCD is directly caused by stress or trauma. However, it *is* true that stress can make OCD symptoms worse.

Hoarding

Another behavior that's often connected to OCD is called hoarding. A million or more people in the United States are hoarders. A person who hoards collects various items in very large amounts. The items themselves often have no real value, such as newspapers or old clothes. But the hoarder is unwilling to get rid of anything.

You might wonder why hoarding is a big deal. Most of us have more "stuff" than we really need. So what if a person wants to collect old newspapers? And you are right—to a point. Some people own more books than they can ever read, or more T-shirts than they can wear. But having a large collection does not make someone a hoarder.

This might look like junk to you, but someone with a hoarding disorder might not be able to get rid of anything.

REASONS PEOPLE HOARD

Everyone is different, and people have different reasons why they collect so much stuff. However, some thought patterns are common among people who hoard.

- **Fear of waste.** They feel guilty about the idea that something might be thrown out that could be used later.
- **Fear of losing information**. They feel worried that a specific book, newspaper, or even junk mail might be needed in the future.
- **Emotional attachment.** They connect specific objects with their feelings about people or events. Getting rid of the object feels like a **betrayal** of the person or memory.
- **Appearance**. They just like the way particular objects look.

(Adapted from "About Hoarding," International OCD Foundation, http://www.ocfoundation.org/hoarding/about.aspx)

People with a hoarding disorder do not just collect one thing. And they cannot stop collecting, even when their homes becomes impossible to live in. Some of these people fill entire rooms with things that most people would consider trash. Hallways and doors get blocked with large piles, so that it's difficult to move around the home. Some people have so much "stuff" that they can't sleep in their beds anymore. There is a risk of fire, and even of floors collapsing under the weight of all that "stuff."

Despite these problems, people with hoarding disorder tend to get very upset when someone suggests they get rid of things. They feel very attached to their belongings. And they can't see why others think their "stuff" has no value. To them, it seems very important.

About three-quarters of people with hoarding disorder also have some other mental disorder. In the next chapter, we will talk about situations where someone with an OCD-related disorder has another problem as well.

Text-Dependent Questions

1. What are the OCD-related disorders that involve the body?
2. What do we know about why these disorders might occur? What do we not know?
3. Why is hoarding a problem?
4. What are some of the reasons people give to explain their hoarding?

Research Project

Pick the disorder in this chapter that is most interesting to you, and find out more about it. Why do people develop this disorder, and what can be done to help them? You might start your search online at sites like the International OCD Foundation (http://www.ocd.org), which has pages on a wide variety of OCD-related disorders.

CHAPTER THREE

OCD AND OTHER DISORDERS

Words to Understand

comorbidity: the presence of more than one disorder in the same person.

grimacing: making unpleasant faces.

motor: having to do with motion; can refer to an actual machine but can also refer to motions of the body.

vocal: having to do with the voice.

Have you ever overslept on a school day? You wake up late, so you have to rush around—getting dressed, packing your books, and finding your sneakers. Being late makes you nervous, and when you're nervous, it gets harder to remember where you left your sneakers. Suddenly you have two problems at the same time, and each one makes the other worse. The first problem is being late, which makes it harder for you to find your sneakers. And the second problem is finding your sneakers, which makes you even later because you spend time hunting for them.

A doctor might say that your lateness is **comorbid** with your missing sneakers.

The word *comorbid* is a bit confusing, because *morbid* sounds like it must have something to do with death. But in fact, *comorbid* just means having more than one illness at the same time. For example, strep (a throat infection) can be comorbid with bronchitis (a lung infection). Mental disorders can also be comorbid with one another. In fact, it is very common for OCD-related disorders to be comorbid with some other problem.

Anxiety and OCD

Anxiety disorders are often comorbid with OCD. It is easy to understand why this might happen. If you have a compulsion about checking your homework a certain number of times, but your parents are telling you to go to bed, you are going to feel anxious. Your OCD wants you to do one thing, and your parents want you to do another, and you are caught in the middle. And just like our example with the sneakers, one problem (the OCD) makes the other problem (anxiety) worse.

Opposite page: It is common for people with OCD to be very anxious. Sometimes it's difficult to tell which came first—the anxiety or the OCD symptoms.

A doctor who is treating a patient with both OCD and anxiety will consider how to help both sets of symptoms. For instance, learning how to relax can help a person with both anxiety and OCD.

Usually, when people with OCD go to mental health professionals, their OCD is the primary problem. So the person and the doctor will probably work on that first. But many of the techniques they learn, and even specific medications they may take, also help with anxiety. When the primary problem is stabilized, people with both OCD and anxiety might start to work more generally on anxiety, too.

Tics and OCD

Tics are repeated body movements or sounds. There are two types: **motor** and **vocal**. Blinking more than necessary,

Relaxation techniques that help with anxiety may also help ease OCD symptoms.

TOURETTE'S DISORDER AND OCD

The most severe type of tic disorder is called Tourette's disorder (also called Tourette's syndrome). The name comes from the French doctor Georges Gilles de la Tourette, who named the illness in 1885. It is considered the most severe because people with Tourette's have both motor *and* vocal tics. Of this group, some have tics that involve swearing. This is called "coprolalia." The swearing tic gets a lot of media attention. Lots of people think that all people with Tourette's swear a lot. But in fact, only 10 to 15 percent of patients with Tourette's have coprolalia.

Sometimes it's very clear that something is a tic. For instance, a person who clears her throat over and over probably has a tic. But what about the person who feels compelled to touch something over and over? Is that a motor tic or is that OCD? The line is not always clear. Even experts on mental disorders may not always agree. The name "Tourettic OCD" reflects this blend of symptoms.

twitching your shoulder, or **grimacing** a lot are simple motor tics. Clearing your throat, coughing, or shouting something you don't really mean is a vocal tic. Tics are fairly common among kids, and lots of kids just grow out of them in time. But some can be so intense that they are called tic disorders.

Most people with tics are able to stop themselves from doing the action for a certain period of time. But holding back on a tic can make a person feel very uncomfortable. And the discomfort just builds and builds until the tic wins out. That relieves the bad feelings for a while, but then the cycle starts over again.

As we've discussed, OCD works in a similar way. Someone with a compulsion can often resist that urge for a time, but sooner or later the pressure becomes too much. This may be why many people who have OCD also have tics. In fact, sometimes it is difficult for doctors to tell whether someone has one or the other disorder.

Depression and Hoarding

Two other disorders—depression and the hoarding type of OCD—often occur together. Our understanding of hoarding is fairly new—it has only been viewed as a distinct disorder for a short time. For that reason, few researchers have studied why the two disorders occur together in so many people. It may be that collecting things cheers up some depressed people. Getting something new might make a person feel better for a short period of time.

Another possible reason is indecision. Being depressed makes it much harder for people to make choices. Depressed people might hoard objects rather than decide to throw things out.

COMORBIDITY AND OCD

In addition to the pairings discussed here, OCD can also be comorbid with other disorders, including the following:

- autism spectrum disorders
- attention-deficit hyperactivity disorder
- bipolar disorder
- disruptive behavior disorders
- panic disorder
- schizophrenia
- social anxiety

These problems are all discussed in other volumes in this set.

Buying new things might make a depressed person feel better for a short time, but the feelings don't usually last for very long.

Body Dysmorphia and Anorexia

The word *dysmorphia* comes from a similar-sounding Greek word, *dusmorphia*, which means "ugliness." Chapter two discusses body dysmorphic disorder (BDD) and how persons with BDD are convinced that something about their body is ugly.

A milder version of this problem is just called body dysmorphia. It is very common among people with the eating disorder called anorexia. People with anorexia keep dieting even when they are extremely thin. When they look in the

The type of OCD called body dysmorphia often goes hand-in-hand with eating disorders.

mirror, anorexic people often see themselves as fat, no matter how thin they are. As with OCD, they can't seem to "know" that they are actually thin.

Text-dependent Questions

1. What does comorbid mean? Give an example.
2. What disorders are often comorbid with OCD?
3. What is Tourette's disorder?

Research Project

Find out more about the history of Tourette's disorder. Why do you think this disorder and OCD so often occur together?

CHAPTER FOUR

TREATING OCD

Words to Understand

cognitive: having to do with the mind and thoughts.

exposure: experiencing something.

insight: understanding of a particular idea or situation.

response: an answer or reaction to something.

technique: a way to do something or to accomplish a task.

You probably do homework every night. You sit down at a desk or table and work on the assignment until it's done. Then you put the homework away and do something else. Some kids with OCD can't do that so easily. They might feel compelled to check and recheck the same homework

HIDDEN OCD

It can be hard to tell whether someone is struggling with intrusive thoughts. Here are a few ways that OCD symptoms can hide themselves:

- **Doing simple things slowly.** People with OCD often worry about doing things "perfectly," which can slow them down. Getting dressed, doing homework, or taking tests can take much longer.

- **Visiting the bathroom a lot.** If someone with OCD has a ritual that involves hand-washing or cleaning, he may take a long time in the bathroom and need to visit it often.

- **Starting things over.** When a ritual gets interrupted, the person with OCD will probably need to start it over again.

- **Avoiding certain numbers.** A person with OCD might refuse to sit in the fifth row of the bus, or he may avoid a locker number with a four in it. These refusals might be confusing to others, but they make sense to the person with the disorder—his OCD is telling him that the number is bad or unlucky.

- **Difficulty making decisions.** Having OCD can make it very hard for someone to make what seem like simple choices.

assignment for hours. As mentioned in chapter one, even though they can *see* that their homework is done, a part of their brains does not truly "know" that it's done. So they have to keep checking it.

These kinds of behaviors sometimes make others believe that people with OCD are not very smart. But that's not true! Having OCD does not mean you aren't smart. It just means that you need to learn how to "know" the things that other people take for granted. This is where medicine and therapy can help.

It's common for people with OCD to be tired a lot; rituals can make it hard to get a good night's sleep.

Admitting the Problem

Many people with OCD secretly know that something is wrong. This is called having **insight** into their condition.

YOU AREN'T WEIRD!

Having insight into your disorder is great. It makes treatment easier and recovery more likely. But insight can have a down side as well.

People with OCD who have good insight are well aware that their rituals are not "normal." They feel ashamed about the "strange" things they do. So they tend to keep their rituals a secret. It can take people with OCD many years to find the courage to tell the truth.

It's important to remember that having OCD does not make you "weird" or "crazy." Your brain is just different from other people's. Some people say it's kind of like a brain "hiccup," or having your brain stuck on repeat. And you need some help to learn how to do the regular things that other people do every day. But you can't get that help if you don't ask. If you have rituals or compulsions that make you upset, tell a trusted adult.

Doctors talk about three levels of insight: good, poor, and absent. Let's use the young man checking his locked door as an example.

- **Good insight** means he understands that nothing bad is likely to happen if he doesn't check the door.
- **Poor insight** means he *thinks* something bad might happen, but he isn't completely sure.
- **Absent insight** means he is completely sure that his family will be killed if the door is not checked.

The more insight he has, the more willing he will be to listen to the advice of a therapist on how to stop.

Levels of insight vary. And people with certain types of OCD tend to have better insight than others. People who are compelled to wash, arrange, or check on things often have pretty good insight. People with hoarding and body dysmorphic disorders, meanwhile, tend to have much less insight about their problems.

Treatments: Medication

There are medicines that can help some people with OCD. These drugs, such as fluoxetine (also called Prozac), help adjust the chemistry of the brain. And these changes in chemistry can help lessen the compulsions that people with OCD feel.

HELPING SOMEONE WITH OCD

If you have a friend or relative who has OCD, here are some things you can do to help:

- *Learn to spot the signals* that the person is having trouble.
- Try to *lower your expectations* for that person if he or she is stressed.
- Recognize *small improvements*. What seems easy for you may be a big deal for someone with OCD.
- Keep your *communication clear and simple*.
- *Be sensitive* to the person's mood, and to whether this is an anxious day or a less-anxious day.
- If today is an anxious day, try to *be flexible* with your plans.
- *Be good to yourself*, too! It's not easy having a friend or family member with OCD.

Some people don't like taking medication because of the side effects, or because they fear that the drugs will change their personalities. But the correct dose of the right medication can make a person with OCD feel much better, and it doesn't need to change who the person is.

Having OCD can make it hard to sleep or do well in school. It can make it hard to have friends, because other kids may not understand why someone with OCD has these rituals. Another reason to prescribe medicine is if the OCD is comorbid with some other disorder, as discussed in chapter three.

But no pill will make OCD disappear completely. In addition to medicine, most doctors suggest **cognitive**-behavioral therapy (CBT). The key is to learn how to live with the disorder—to manage it, rather than letting it manage you. Most of the time, mental health professionals will recommend trying therapy without medication first. But if things do not start to improve, or if symptoms are so severe that they prevent you from going to school, medicine may help while you learn these new skills.

Treatments: Therapy

CBT is based on the idea that if someone understands why he acts a certain way, he can learn how to have more control over his behavior. People with OCD-related disorders can use CBT to learn the following things:

- *why* they have intrusive thoughts
- *why* they feel certain compulsions
- *what to do* about those thoughts and compulsions

Therapists often use a **technique** called "**exposure** and **response** prevention." First, a therapist works with a patient to make a list of the ideas or situations that produce fear. Then the therapist teaches the patient methods of reducing anxiety. Starting with the item that is the least feared, the therapist will help the patient confront the fear using relaxation techniques. This is called "exposure."

For example, let's consider the young man from chapter one who checks his door. He might be *most* worried about what will happen if he does not check the door, and *least* worried about what will happen if he doesn't check his backpack before bed to be sure everything is in it. The therapist might have him practice *not* checking his backpack,

Mental health professionals can help people with OCD gain control over their intrusive thoughts.

THOUGHTS VERSUS REALITY

People with OCD are somewhat similar to people with anxiety disorders. They need to remember that just because they imagine something *might* happen, that doesn't mean it will. That's easy to say, but not always easy to do.

Put yourself in the shoes of someone who has intrusive thoughts. You believe that if you don't perform a certain ritual, your house could burn down. This belief is very real to you. If you were that person, would you perform the ritual? If you sincerely believed your house was in danger, you probably would!

But *thinking about* the bad thing does not mean the bad thing will happen. This is why behavioral therapy can be so helpful. People can learn to react differently to the thoughts they have.

while using his relaxation strategies. This is exposure to his fear. Most of the time with younger children, parents are also taught these techniques, so they can help the patient practice at home.

Over time, he will gradually realize that nothing bad is going to happen at all. And he will find it easier to resist the compulsion to check the door. Ideally, he will understand that his intrusive thoughts about the door are just that—thoughts. They are not real.

The OCD does not have to be in charge. Getting it under control can take time and practice, but it can be done.

Text-Dependent Questions

1. What does it mean if we say someone has "poor insight" about his or her disorder?

2. What are the two main types of treatments for OCD?

3. How does exposure and response prevention work?

Research Project

Find out more about fluoxetine. How does it work on the brain? What are the possible side effects? Write a brief report, of two to three paragraphs, about it.

"You are not your illness. You have an individual story to tell. You have a name, a history, a personality. Staying yourself is part of the battle."
—Julian Seifter

Further Reading

BOOKS

Colas, Emily. *Just Checking: Scenes from the Life of an Obsessive-Compulsive.* New York: Pocket Books, 1998.

Dotson, Alison. *Being Me with OCD: How I Learned to Obsess Less and Live My Life.* Minneapolis, MN: Free Spirit Publishing, 2014.

Heubner, Dawn. *What to Do When Your Brain Gets Stuck: A Kid's Guide to Overcoming OCD.* Washington, DC: Magination Press, 2007.

March, John S., with Christine M. Benton. *Talking Back to OCD: The Program That Helps Kids and Teens Say "No Way"—and Parents Say "Way to Go."* New York: Guilford Press, 2007.

Philips, Katharine A. *The Broken Mirror: Understanding and Treating Body Dysmorphic Disorder.* New York: Oxford University Press, 2005.

ONLINE

International OCD Foundation. http://www.ocd.org.

KidsHealth. "Obsessive-Compulsive Disorder." http://kidshealth.org/parent/emotions/behavior/OCD.html.

Mayo Clinic. "Obsessive-Compulsive Disorder (OCD)." http://www.mayoclinic.org/diseases-conditions/ocd/basics/definition/con-20027827.

Trichotillomania Learning Center. http://www.trich.org/.

LOSING HOPE?

This free, confidential phone number will connect you to counselors who can help.

National Suicide Prevention Lifeline

1-800-273-TALK (1-800-273-8255)

"Mental illness is nothing to be ashamed of, but stigma and bias shame us all. Together, we will replace stigma with acceptance, ignorance with understanding, fear with new hope for the future. Together, we will build a stronger nation for the new century, leaving no one behind."
—Bill Clinton

Series Glossary

acute: happening powerfully for a short period of time.

affect: as a noun, the way someone seems on the outside—including attitude, emotion, and voice (pronounced with the emphasis on the first syllable, "AFF-eckt").

atypical: different from what is usually expected.

bipolar: involving two, opposite ends.

chronic: happening again and again over a long period of time.

comorbidity: two or more illnesses appearing at the same time.

correlation: a relationship or connection.

delusion: a false belief with no connection to reality.

dementia: a mental disorder, featuring severe memory loss.

denial: refusal to admit that there is a problem.

depressant: a substance that slows down bodily functions.

depression: a feeling of hopelessness and lack of energy.

deprivation: a hurtful lack of something important.

diagnose: to identify a problem.

empathy: understanding someone else's situation and feelings.

epidemic: a widespread illness.

euphoria: a feeling of extreme, even overwhelming, happiness.

hallucination: something a person sees or hears that is not really there.

heredity: the passing of a trait from parents to children.

hormone: a substance in the body that helps it function properly.

hypnotic: a type of drug that causes sleep.

impulsivity: the tendency to act without thinking.

inattention: distraction; not paying attention.

insomnia: inability to fall asleep and/or stay asleep.

licensed: having an official document proving one is capable with a certain set of skills.

manic: a high level of excitement or energy.

misdiagnose: to incorrectly identify a problem.

moderation: limited in amount, not extreme.

noncompliance: refusing to follow rules or do as instructed.

onset: the beginning of something; pronounced like "on" and "set."

outpatient: medical care that happens while a patient continues to live at home.

overdiagnose: to determine more people have a certain illness than actually do.

pediatricians: doctors who treat children and young adults.

perception: awareness or understanding of reality.

practitioner: a person who actively participates in a particular field.

predisposition: to be more likely to do something, either due to your personality or biology.

psychiatric: having to do with mental illness.

psychiatrist: a medical doctor who specializes in mental disorders.

psychoactive: something that has an effect on the mind and behavior.

psychosis: a severe mental disorder where the person loses touch with reality.

psychosocial: the interaction between someone's thoughts and the outside world of relationships.

psychotherapy: treatment for mental disorders.

relapse: getting worse after a period of getting better.

spectrum: a range; in medicine, from less extreme to more extreme.

stereotype: a simplified idea about a type of person, not connected to actual individuals.

stimulant: a substance that speeds up bodily functions.

therapy: treatment of a problem; can be done with medicine or simply by talking with a therapist.

trigger: something that causes something else.

Index

Page numbers in *italics* refer to photographs.

About the Author

H. W. POOLE is a writer and editor of books for young people, such as the *Horrors of History* series (Charlesbridge). She is also responsible for many critically acclaimed reference books, including *Political Handbook of the World* (CQ Press) and the *Encyclopedia of Terrorism* (SAGE). She was coauthor and editor of the *History of the Internet* (ABC-CLIO), which won the 2000 American Library Association RUSA award.

About the Advisor

ANNE S. WALTERS is Clinical Associate Professor of Psychiatry and Human Behavior. She is the Clinical Director of the Children's Partial Hospital Program at Bradley Hospital, a program that provides partial hospital level of care for children ages 7–12 and their families. She also serves as Chief Psychologist for Bradley Hospital. She is actively involved in teaching activities within the Clinical Psychology Training Programs of the Alpert Medical School of Brown University and serves as Child Track Seminar Co-Coordinator. Dr. Walters completed her undergraduate work at Duke University, graduate school at Georgia State University, internship at UTexas Health Science Center, and postdoctoral fellowship at Brown University. Her interests lie in the area of program development, treatment of severe psychiatric disorders in children, and psychotic spectrum disorders.

Photo Credits

Photos are for illustrative purposes only; individuals depicted in the photos, both on the cover and throughout this book, are only models.

Cover Photo: iStock.com/jorgeantonio

Dollar Photo Club: 10 elenarostunova; 11 Lubos Chlubny; 13 xy; 15 Monkey Business; 21 wusuowei; 22 Africa Studio; 23 Gry Thunes; 27 Sabphoto; 28 Baronb; 31 carol_anne; 34 Ken Hurst. **iStock.com:** 14 sumnersgraphicsinc; 16 monkeybusinessimages; 19 JENasir; 20 coward_lion; 32 PeopleImages; 35 monkeybusinessimages; 37 prudkov; 39 monkeybusinessimages; 40 Cimmerian. **Library of Congress:** 12.